W9-CQB-064

SCIENCE WORKSHOP

AIR · WIND & FLIGHT

Mick Seller

SHOOTING STAR PRESS

This edition produced in **1993** for
Shooting Star Press Inc
230 Fifth Avenue
New York, NY 10001

© Aladdin Books Ltd 1992

All rights reserved

Printed in Belgium

Created and produced by
NW Books
28 Percy Street
London W1P 9FF

Design	David West Children's Book Design
Editors	Catherine Warren, Michael Flaherty
Designer	John Kelly
Picture Researcher	Emma Krikler
Illustrator	Ian Thompson
Consultant	Geoff Leyland

First published in the
United States in 1992 by
Gloucester Press

ISBN 1-56924-008-6

CONTENTS

PHOTOCREDITS

All the pictures in this book have been taken by Roger Viltos apart from the pictures on pages: 8 top left, 12 top left, 14 top right, 16 top right, 18 top left,22 top left and 26 left: Spectrum Colour Library; page 10 top left: Lycoming Pratt and Witney; pages 12 top right, 14 top left, 16 top left and 20 left and right: Eye Ubiquuitous; page 30 top left and top right: Aladdin's Lamp; page 28 top; The Ministry of Defence.

INTRODUCTION

Air is all around us. Even though we cannot see it, taste it, or grab hold of it, air is essential to life on Earth. Invisible air is not empty space. It is actually a rich mix of many different gases, including the oxygen that we breathe. The blanket of air surrounding our planet is thick and heavy. Indeed, the force of air pressure pushes on us from every direction. We can measure slight air changes in this pressure to forecast the weather. Movements of hot and cold air, which make nature's gentle breezes and fierce hurricanes, can be utilized to launch a hot air balloon. Changes in air pressure, made by the delicate curve of a wing, make flight possible, while the force of air resistance, captured with a parachute, cushions a landing. The power of wind can be trapped by windmills to drive machines, and sails to propel boats. The gases in the atmosphere can be compressed to fit into a smaller volume. This allows large amounts of air to be stored, for example, in small metal cylinders such as the aqualungs used by divers to breathe underwater. Plentiful and fascinating, air promises science and technology new discoveries for centuries to come.

Bright Ideas for
further projects

Introduction

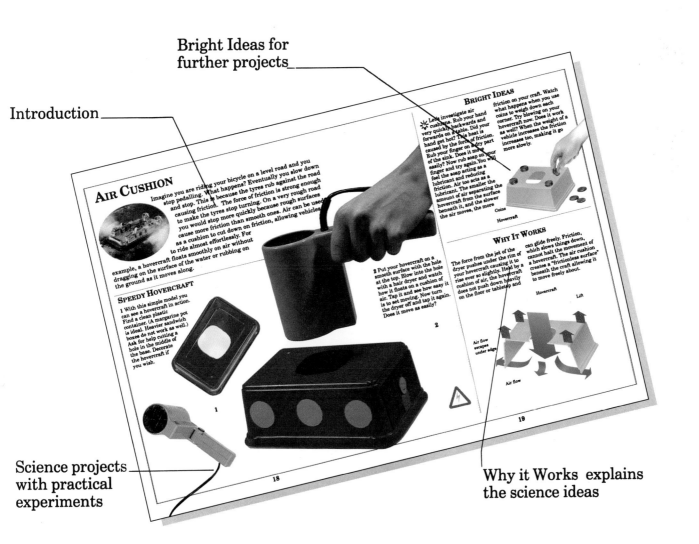

Science projects
with practical
experiments

Why it Works explains
the science ideas

THE WORKSHOP

A science workshop is a place to test ideas, perform experiments, and make discoveries. To prove many scientific facts you don't need a lot of fancy equipment. In fact, everything you need for a basic workshop can be found around your home or school. Read through these pages and then use your imagination to add to your "home laboratory." Make sure that you are aware of relevant safety rules and look after the environment. A science experiment is an activity that involves the use of certain basic rules to test a hypothesis. A qualitative approach involves observation. A quantitative approach involves measurement. Remember, one of the keys to being a creative scientist is to keep experimenting. This means experimenting with equipment as well as with ideas and building up your workshop as you go.

Making the Models

Before you begin, read through all the steps. Then make a list of the things you need and gather them together. Next, think about the project so that you have a clear idea of what you are about to do. Finally, take your time in putting the pieces together. You will find that your projects work best if you wait while glue dries or water heats. If something goes wrong, retrace your steps. And, if you can't fix it, start over. Every scientist makes mistakes, but the best ones know when to begin again.

General Tips

There are at least two parts to every experiment: experimenting with materials and testing a science "fact." If you don't have all the materials, experiment with others instead. For example, try a plastic soda bottle if you can't find a dishwashing liquid container. Once you've finished experimenting, read your notes thoroughly and think about what happened. See what conclusions you can draw from your results.

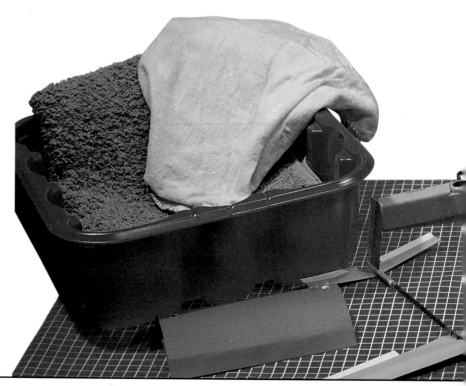

Experimenting

Always conduct a careful test. Change only one thing at a time for each stage of an experiment. In this way you can always test which change caused a different result. Make complete notes as you go along. Ask questions such as "why?," "how?," and "what if?" Then test your model and write down your answers.

Safety Warnings

Many of these experiments use a hair dryer. Always be careful when plugging and unplugging it. Never use a hair dryer near water. Don't keep it on for too long or it may overheat. Experiments with candles should be done with an adult. Don't leave your equipment on a radiator. Clean up when you finish!

ESSENTIAL OXYGEN

Everything around us is either solid, a liquid, or a gas. Gases are the lightest (or least dense) of all. Solid things, like cars, can move through gases. The air around us is a mixture of gases. Most of the air, about four-fifths, is nitrogen. About one fifth is oxygen. Then there are small amounts of other gases, argon, helium, krypton, xenon, neon, and carbon dioxide. Finally, there is some water vapor in the air. Without oxygen we could not breathe, and without oxygen fires would not burn – like us they would suffocate. In about 1670 the English doctor John Mayow proved that fire consumes air. By repeating his experiment, you can also see how a flame uses up a part of the air.

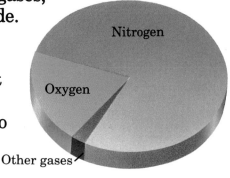

Nitrogen

Oxygen

Other gases

"BREATHING" FIRE

1 To test that fire actually burns air, you need a few household items. Find a bowl made of something that is fireproof (not plastic), three coins, a clean glass jar, modeling clay, and a candle.

2 Push a small lump of clay onto the middle of the bowl. Arrange the coins so that the top of the jar will rest on them without wobbling. Firmly push the candle into the clay and half fill the bowl with water.

3 Ask an adult to help you with this step. Light the candle and then very carefully lower the glass jar over the flame, resting it on the coins. Quickly mark the water level on the side of the jar. Watch the flame closely to see how it changes.

1

2

3

WHY IT WORKS

The flame uses up the oxygen in the air as it burns. Once much of the oxygen is taken up, there is no longer enough to support a flame and the candle goes out. Air pressure (see pages 8, 9) pushes on the water outside the jar. Inside the jar, the water is forced into the space left by the oxygen. The water level inside rises by about one-fifth, the fraction of oxygen in the air.

This experiment is not exact. Some of the air escapes from the jar as the flame burns because air expands when heated. As the air cools down it shrinks, or contracts, making extra space for the water to fill.

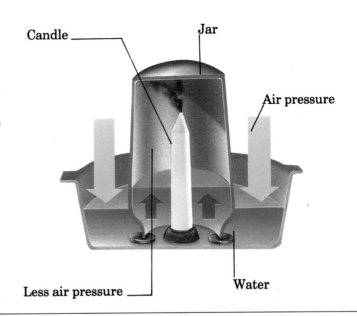

Candle — Jar

Air pressure

Less air pressure — Water

---

4 Note what happens to the water at the bottom of the bowl. As the candle burns notice if bubbles appear. When the candle goes out see if the water level rises inside the jar. Observe how high it has risen. Mark the side of the glass to show the new water level.

BRIGHT IDEAS

Light two candles. Cover one with a small jar and one with a large jar. See which candle burns the longest.

Place a dried pea into the neck of a bottle. Blow hard to make the pea go into the bottle. Notice whether the air pressure inside the bottle is strong enough to keep the pea out.

4

POWERFUL PRESSURE

Although we don't really notice it much, the air is all around us and is pressing on us all the time. Air pressure is caused because air has weight and it is pulled down to Earth by gravity. As it is pulled down it squeezes against things – this is air pressure. Our own blood pressure presses back against the air – if we suddenly took air pressure away, our bodies would explode. This is why spacemen have to wear special pressurized suits: in space there is no air and so no air pressure. Slight changes in air pressure give us a clue about weather changes. We can measure air pressure and so predict the weather with an instrument called a barometer.

WEATHER FORECASTING

1 You can make a simple barometer by using a new balloon, a clean glass jar, a straw, a toothpick, a rubber band, oak tag, and some cardboard. Cut the neck off the balloon. Stretch the balloon over the jar. Hold it in place with the rubber band.

2 Tape the toothpick to the end of the straw. Tape the other end of the straw to the center of the balloon lid. Make a weather picture chart on the oak tag, with the good weather at the top.

3 Fold the sheet of oak tag and cut a cardboard triangle for a support. Fix the weather chart in position. Put the barometer in place and watch the pointer move a little each day.

WHY IT WORKS

Air pressure changes all the time. It pushes on us from all directions because of the endless jostling of gas molecules. When the air pressure rises, indicating good weather, the pressure pushes down on your barometer's lid, making the straw pointer rise. When the air pressure drops, indicating bad weather, the lid swells and the pointer drops. Air temperature also affects pressure. Your barometer is most accurate when kept at a steady temperature.

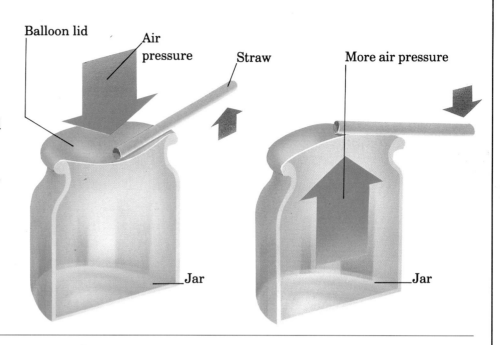

Balloon lid

Air pressure

Straw

More air pressure

Jar

Jar

BRIGHT IDEAS

Try to lift a piece of paper from a tabletop using only a ruler as in the picture. Feel the air pressure try to stop you.

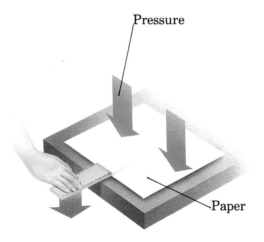

Pressure

Paper

Very carefully hang a ruler from its center by a string so that it balances perfectly. Take two identical balloons and blow one up. Tape the balloons to either end of the ruler. You'll need identical pieces of tape to keep the experiment fair. Notice what happens. Which balloon is the heaviest and why?

Empty balloon

Full balloon

RISING CURRENTS

Have you ever wondered what makes the wind blow? As the air is warmed by the sun it expands and becomes lighter. These changes cause the warm air to rise. At the same time, cooler air moves in, filling up the space left behind. So, the air is moving, and moving air is wind. The rotation of the earth complicates the pattern, causing wind to swirl. Satellite images of the earth show the clouds above us in constant motion due to these air currents.

Mobile Air

1

1 You can prove that hot air rises with a mobile that spins in the slightest current. Cut some shapes from aluminum foil. For the mobile shown here you need two squares and two circles.

2

2 Turn one of the circles into a spiral like a snail's shell. Make a pinwheel using one of the squares. Twist and cut the other two pieces using your imagination to make interesting shapes. With a needle, thread a length of cotton through each one.

3

3 Cut a triangle from a piece of cardboard. Decorate one side and tape a stick securely to the other to make the stand. Attach a piece of clay to the bottom of the stick. Make sure the complete stand balances upright evenly.

4

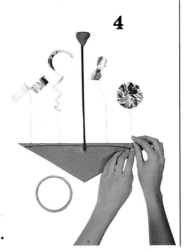

4 Carefully tape the thread lengths to the back of the triangle. Make sure each shape can twist freely. Place your mobile above a radiator, keeping it well away from gas and fire and breezes. Watch the shapes twirl.

Bright Ideas

The spirals turn very nicely in the currents of rising hot air, but would other shapes turn as well? Try a twisted loop, a circle, a strip. Notice which works best. Are the best shapes similar to birds' feathers or the wings of a glider? Do the spirals work better with longer or shorter strings? Is close to the radiator best, or high above it?

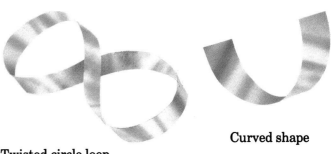

Curved shape

Twisted circle loop

Why It Works

Although dangling at rest when placed elsewhere in a room, your mobile shapes twirl when hung above a radiator. This is because rising warm air pushes upward on the edges of the shapes, causing them to twist and turn like a propeller.

The movements of hot and cold air are called convection currents and cause many winds. The hottest part of the earth is the equator – here the air is heated and it rises. High in the air it travels out toward the poles. At the cold North and South poles the air cools and falls, then travels toward the equator.

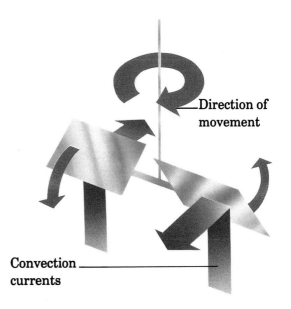

Direction of movement

Convection currents

HOT-AIR FLIGHT

Have you seen a hot-air balloon? More than 200 years ago, two French brothers, Joseph and Jacques Montgolfier, discovered that rising hot air could be captured and used for flight. They made a huge balloon from linen and paper and built a fire underneath it. The balloon trapped the hot air and smoke rising from the fire and lifted the two men into the air. As the air cooled, the balloon floated back down to the ground. Since that first flight, people have used hot-air balloons for pleasure, for racing, and even for warfare. You can make your own hot-air balloon.

BALLOON LIFT-OFF

1

1 To make a balloon that traps hot air to fly, you need four large sheets of tissue paper. Fold each sheet in half and lightly copy this shape on to one using a pencil. When you are happy with the outline cut out your first "panel."

2 Use the first panel to help you mark out the next three. Cut them out and trim them carefully to make sure they are all the same size.

2

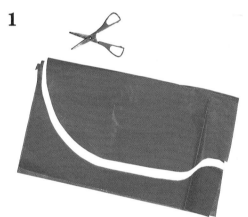

3

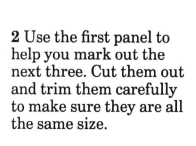

3 Unfold your first panel and spread glue on the edge of one half. Stick the second panel on top and press down. Repeat with the next panel until all four panels are joined into a balloon.

4 Make a small "passenger basket" from a piece of folded oak tag. Attach the basket to the open end of the balloon with four lengths of thread.

4

5 Take the balloon outside for your first flight. Blow up the balloon with hot air from a hair dryer and watch it lift off.

5

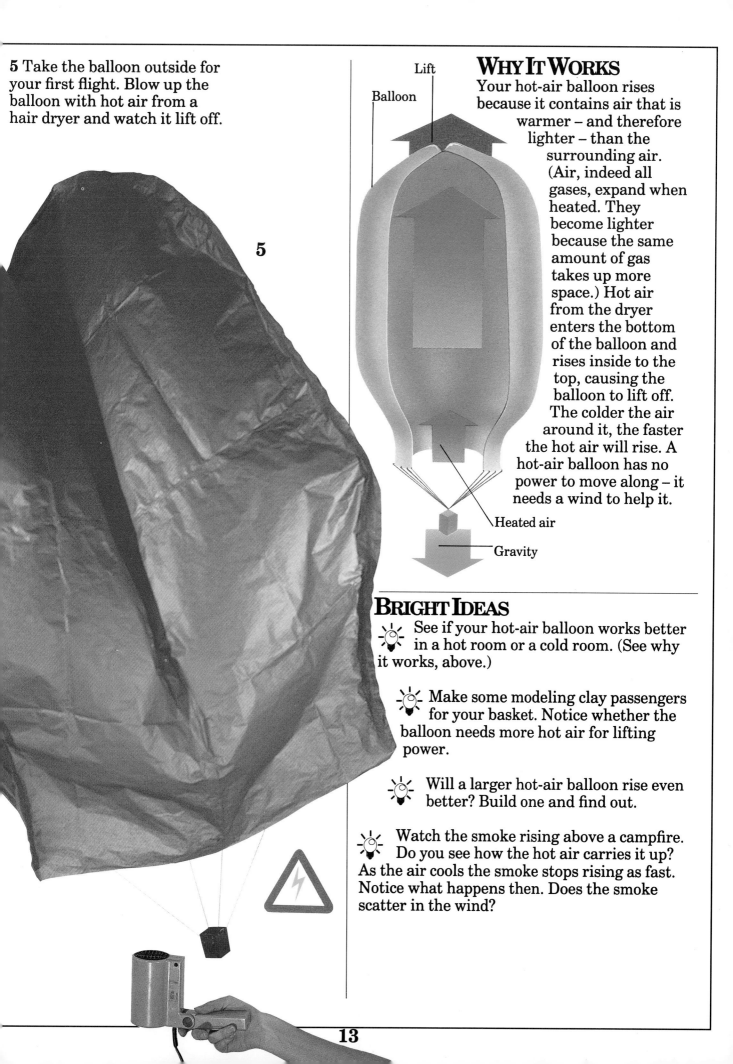

WHY IT WORKS

Your hot-air balloon rises because it contains air that is warmer – and therefore lighter – than the surrounding air. (Air, indeed all gases, expand when heated. They become lighter because the same amount of gas takes up more space.) Hot air from the dryer enters the bottom of the balloon and rises inside to the top, causing the balloon to lift off. The colder the air around it, the faster the hot air will rise. A hot-air balloon has no power to move along – it needs a wind to help it.

Lift

Balloon

Heated air

Gravity

BRIGHT IDEAS

See if your hot-air balloon works better in a hot room or a cold room. (See why it works, above.)

Make some modeling clay passengers for your basket. Notice whether the balloon needs more hot air for lifting power.

Will a larger hot-air balloon rise even better? Build one and find out.

Watch the smoke rising above a campfire. Do you see how the hot air carries it up? As the air cools the smoke stops rising as fast. Notice what happens then. Does the smoke scatter in the wind?

CAPTURING WIND

More than four thousand years ago people were already capturing the wind in sails to move boats through the water. These boats had "square rigged" sails which caught the wind, and oars for rowing when the wind blew the wrong way or when there was no wind at all. About 1,500 years ago, sailors discovered that with a special triangular sail called a "lateen" they could actually sail against the wind. Modern sailboats have tough, nylon sails designed to catch the wind from any angle. A windsurfer's single sail swivels around the board to take the craft in any direction. By trying it out on a simple boat, we can see how a lateen sail works.

5 Fill the bathtub with enough water to float your boat. Place your sailboat in the tub. Use your mouth or a hair dryer at some distance from your boat to blow on the sail, and watch your craft sail away. Both the keel and the rudder keep the boat moving in a straight line.

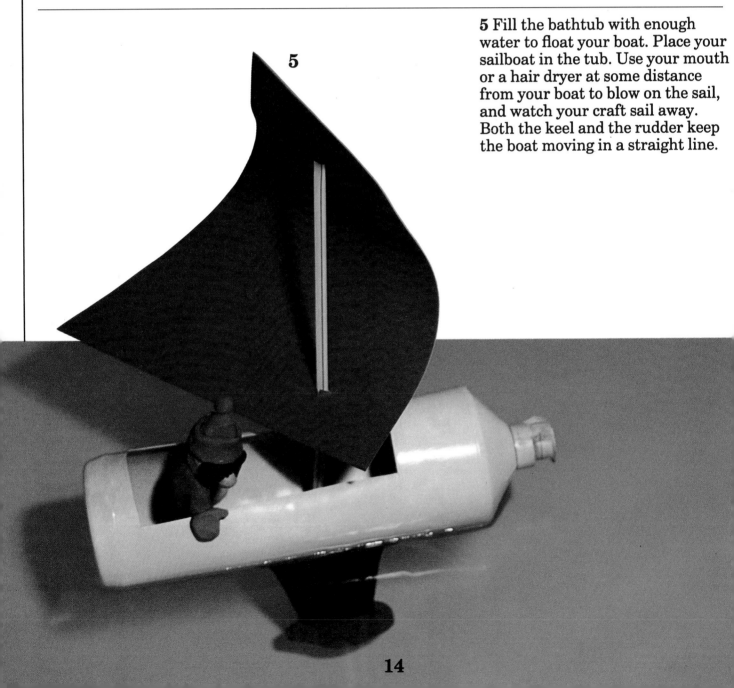

14

SAIL POWER

1 To make a sailboat, first cut a rectangular hole in the side of a plastic bottle.

2 Secure a blob of modeling clay inside the bottle boat. Use it to hold your straw mast in place.

3 Cut a triangle from a piece of paper and decorate it if you wish. Pierce two holes through your sail. Feed the mast through the holes.

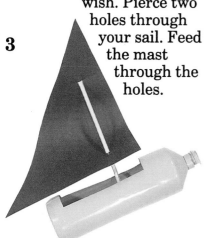

4 Cut a wedge shape from a juice carton for your water-proof keel. Put a chunk of clay on each end and attach it to the boat.

WHY IT WORKS

No matter which way you blow on it, your sailboat can be made to go in any direction. When the wind is directly behind the boat, holding the sail at right angles to the wind channels your boat forward. You can move at right angles, or "across" the wind by again fixing the sail at right angles to the breeze. The boat pictured here is sailing across the wind.

For a "square rigged" boat, the sail is caught in the currents of moving air and pushed along – a bit like you blowing a Ping Pong ball across a table. For a triangular sail the effect is different. The wind blows over the top of the sail and causes low pressure (see pages 18, 19) which sucks the sail, and the boat, forward.

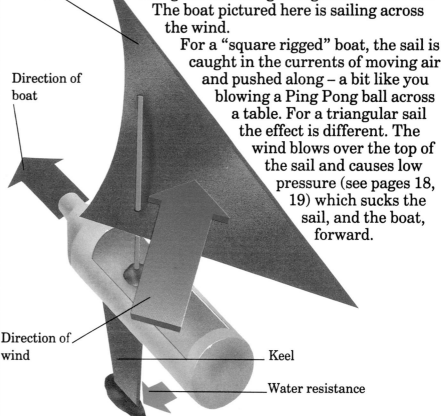

Sail

Direction of boat

Direction of wind

Keel

Water resistance

BRIGHT IDEAS

🔆 Which shape do you think is the best for a sail? Experiment with squares, rectangles, circles, and triangles. Once you've found the best shape, try it out in different sizes. Find out if a smaller sail or a larger sail is the best one.

🔆 Try blowing on your boat from different directions. Watch how the boat moves every time. Now, keeping the "wind" blowing from one direction, see what happens when the sail is fixed as pictured in the two ways below.

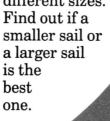

Sail fixed at front of boat

Sail fixed at rear of boat

PRESSURE CHANGES

Even though the rush of wind blows things about, moving air has lower pressure than still air. This is because air molecules have a set amount of energy. When air flows slowly, it has energy left to create sizable pressure. But when air moves quickly, this motion takes up a lot of energy. Therefore, less energy goes into making pressure and the air pressure drops. Because of this, when air moves between things, the air pressure between them is low and the higher surrounding pressure will push them together. Even the tops of tall buildings bow together a little bit on a windy day. This can be illustrated in the project below using simple materials to simulate skyscrapers on a windy day.

BLOWING BALLS

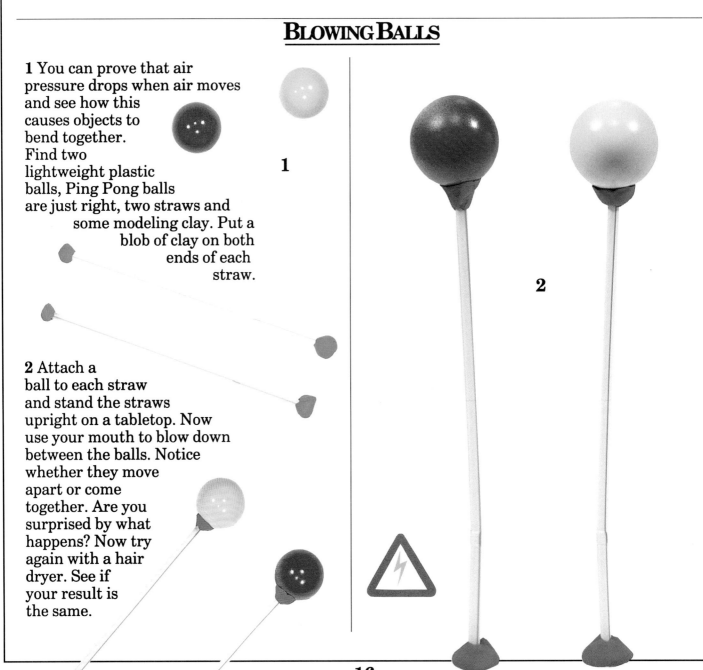

1 You can prove that air pressure drops when air moves and see how this causes objects to bend together. Find two lightweight plastic balls, Ping Pong balls are just right, two straws and some modeling clay. Put a blob of clay on both ends of each straw.

1

2 Attach a ball to each straw and stand the straws upright on a tabletop. Now use your mouth to blow down between the balls. Notice whether they move apart or come together. Are you surprised by what happens? Now try again with a hair dryer. See if your result is the same.

2

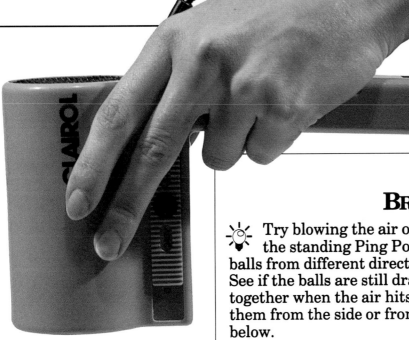

BRIGHT IDEAS

🔆 Try blowing the air onto the standing Ping Pong balls from different directions. See if the balls are still drawn together when the air hits them from the side or from below.

🔆 Hold two strips of paper about 2 inches apart and blow between them. See how the fast moving air pulls the strips inward.

🔆 Hold a strip of paper loosely in front of your mouth and blow over the top. Does the paper rise?

🔆 Cut two small flaps in the end of the strip. Bend one flap down. Blow over the paper again. Notice how the flaps change the paper's motion. Rest a piece of paper over a gap between two books. Blow underneath the paper and watch where it goes.

🔆 Place a small cardboard disk on a table and see if you can lift it simply by blowing over the top.

WHY IT WORKS

When you direct fast moving air between the balls they come together. This is known as the "Bernoulli effect," named after the Swiss mathematician David Bernoulli. More than 250 years ago, he discovered that when water is forced through a constriction in a pipe, its speed increases, but its pressure drops.

Fast moving air has low pressure, too. As you squeeze fast moving air past the two balls it makes a low pressure pocket between them. The "high pressure" air on either side of the balls pushes them into this pocket, thrusting them together.

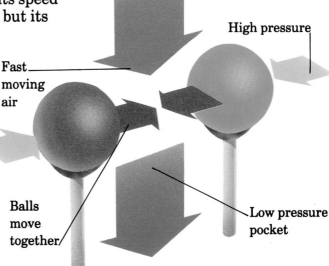

High pressure

Fast moving air

Balls move together

Low pressure pocket

AIR CUSHION

Imagine you are riding your bicycle on a level road and you stop pedaling. What happens? Eventually you slow down and stop. This is because the tires rub against the road, causing friction. The force of friction is strong enough to make the tires stop turning. On a very rough road you would stop more quickly because rough surfaces cause more friction than smooth ones. Air can be used as a cushion to cut down on friction, allowing vehicles to ride almost effortlessly. For example, a hovercraft floats smoothly on air without dragging on the surface of the water or rubbing on the ground as it moves along.

SPEEDY HOVERCRAFT

1 With this simple model you can see a hovercraft in action. Find a clean plastic container. (A margarine tub is ideal. Heavier sandwich boxes do not work as well.) Ask for help cutting a hole in the middle of the base. Decorate the hovercraft if you wish.

1

BRIGHT IDEAS

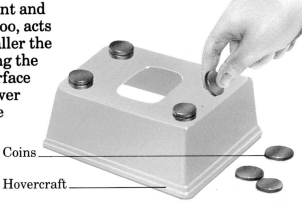

Let's investigate air cushions. Rub your hand very quickly back and forth on a table. Your hand will get hot. This heat is caused by the force of friction. Rub your finger on a dry part of the sink. Does it move easily? Now rub soap on your finger and try again. You will feel the soap acting as a lubricant and reducing friction. Air, too, acts as a lubricant. The smaller the amount of air separating the hovercraft from the surface beneath it, and the slower the air moves, the more friction on your craft. Watch what happens when you use coins to weigh down each corner. Try blowing on your hovercraft now. Does it work as well? When the weight of a vehicle increases the friction increases, too, making it go more slowly.

Coins _____

Hovercraft _____

2 Put your hovercraft on a smooth surface with the hole at the top. Blow into the hole with a hair dryer and watch how it floats on a cushion of air. Tap it and see how easy it is to start moving. Now turn the dryer off and tap it again. Does it move as easily?

WHY IT WORKS

The force from the jet of the dryer pushes under the rim of your hovercraft, causing it to rise ever so slightly. Held by a cushion of air, the hovercraft does not push down heavily on the floor or tabletop and can glide freely. Friction, which slows things down, cannot halt the movement of a hovercraft. The air cushion creates a "frictionless surface" beneath the craft, allowing it to move about freely.

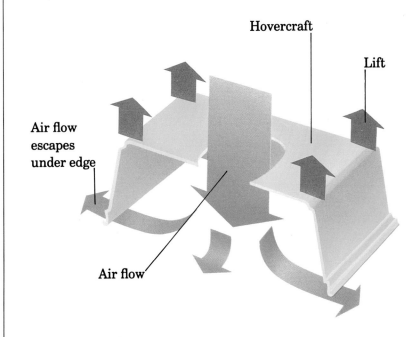

Hovercraft

Lift

Air flow escapes under edge

Air flow

AIR RESISTANCE

If you open an umbrella and try to run with it on a calm day, you will find it difficult as the umbrella captures the air like a parachute, dragging you back. Whenever we move we have to push the air out of the way and we experience air resistance. Sometimes air resistance is helpful, for example in slowing down a parachute. It becomes a nuisance when it acts against a sports car. Some shapes are "streamlined" to move smoothly through the air. They experience less air resistance because the air does not rub against them too much and block their movement.

STREAMLINED SHAPES

1 You can test the force of air resistance. To make a fair test you need two of the same model cars. Make sure their wheels turn freely.

2 Cut two rectangles from a piece of cardboard. Again, to keep the test fair, make them the same size and shape.

3

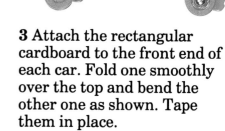

3 Attach the rectangular cardboard to the front end of each car. Fold one smoothly over the top and bend the other one as shown. Tape them in place.

1

2

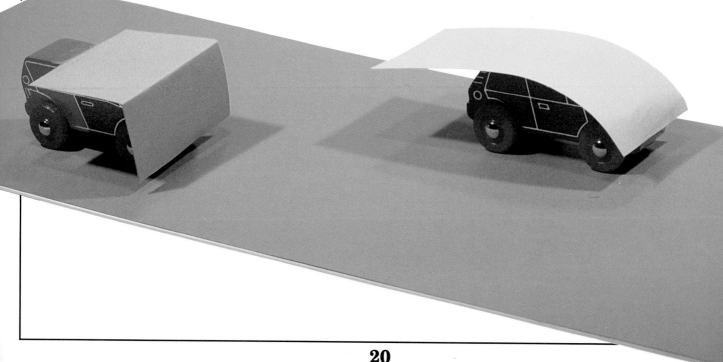

WHY IT WORKS

The shape of your cars makes them roll quickly or slowly. Air flows smoothly over the car with the rounded paper front. This streamlining allows it to roll faster than the car with the square front, which is held back by air resistance, or drag. Drag slows things down, creating ripples of air behind them. These moving ripples, or eddies, lower the air pressure behind the unstreamlined car, keeping it back as it moves.

Air moves over easily

Streamlined shape

Drag

Square front

Ripples of air

4

4 Tilt a board on a book to form a ramp. Release the cars at the same time from the top of the ramp into a wind from a hair dryer. Notice which one experiences least air resistance.

BRIGHT IDEAS

Capture air with a simple parachute. Tie four strings to the corners of a large handkerchief. Fix a blob of modeling clay to the strings. Now make a larger parachute from paper, attaching the same piece of clay. It will drop more slowly than the first one because it captures more air.

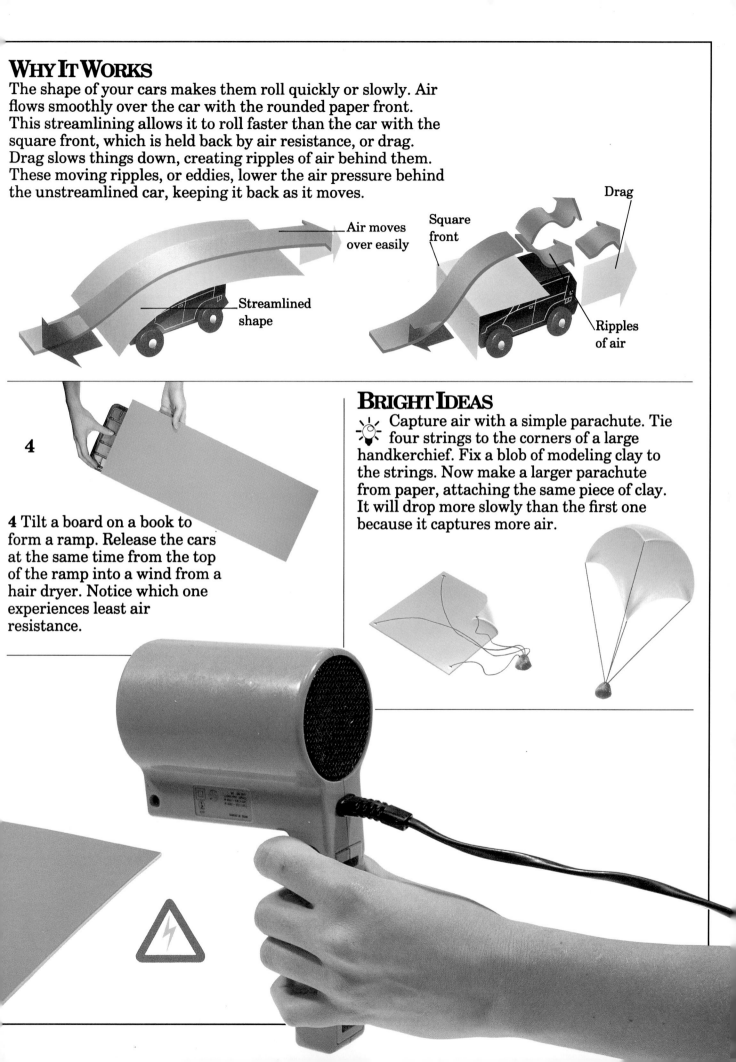

WINGS IN FLIGHT

Birds, insects, bats, and airplanes all need wings to fly. When the Wright brothers made the first powered flight in 1903, it was after years of studying nature's wings. Whether wings are made of something as light as feather or as rigid as metal, it is their shape that gives them lift. This special wing shape is known as an airfoil. Flat on the bottom and curved on top, the airfoil cuts through the air, creating low pressure above which helps the airfoil to rise. You can demonstrate this in the project below.

AIRFOIL

1 To make your own flying wing you need a piece of oak tag measuring about 4in by 6in. Fold the oak tag in two, leaving an overlap of about ½in.

1

2 Push the overlapping ends together. This will make one side of the folded paper curve up. Tape it in place.

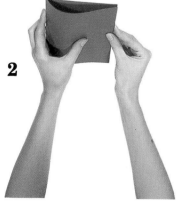

2

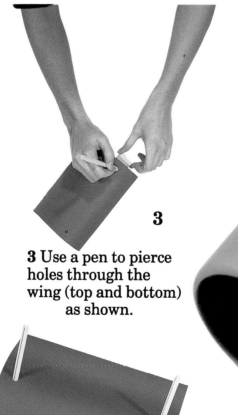

3

3 Use a pen to pierce holes through the wing (top and bottom) as shown.

4

4 Carefully push a drinking straw through each set of holes.

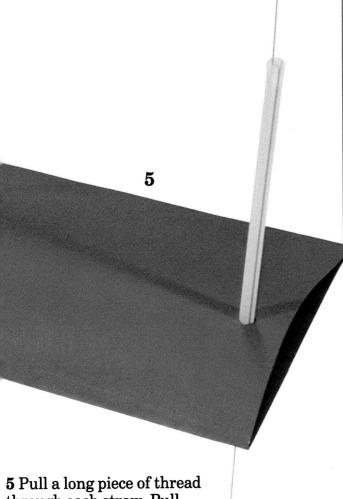

5 Pull a long piece of thread through each straw. Pull these tracks tight and fix them straight between a floor and table, so the wing can slide up and down freely. Lift the wing up a little and aim a hair dryer at the folded edge. Turn the dryer on, and watch your wing soar. Make sure you are pointing the dryer straight for the best lift.

BRIGHT IDEAS

Turn your airfoil upside down and test it again. Notice what happens now. Move the hair dryer back from your airfoil. Does it stay up? See how far back you can move the hair dryer before the airfoil drops down.

Make another airfoil double the size. It creates lower pressure above. Try to move the hair dryer even further away.

Larger airfoil

First airfoil

WHY IT WORKS

Your airfoil rises because of its shape. The top surface of the wing is longer than the bottom surface. Air passing over the top of the wing has farther to travel – so it has to go faster. Faster moving air has lower pressure. (Remember the Bernoulli effect!) Low pressure above the wing causes it to lift.

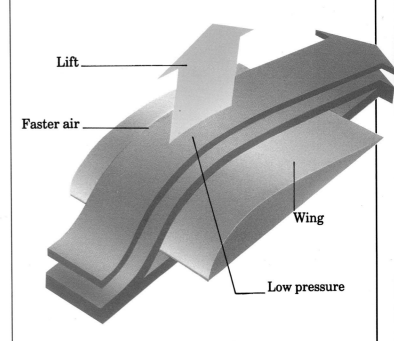

Lift

Faster air

Wing

Low pressure

Airstream Evidence

Some things are shaped to move through the air very smoothly, such as rockets, airplanes, and racing cars. Can you think of any more?

Designers use a wind tunnel to test streamlined shapes. Streams of smoke are blown over new models to show how air currents move around them. The flow of smoke tells designers how much air resistance their vehicles will have to face. The straighter the flow of smoke – the less it curls when it hits a surface – the more streamlined the shape is and the better it will move through the air.

Fast moving shapes are also slowed down by drag. The faster a car or an aircraft moves, the more that drag holds it back. A low drag shape in a wind tunnel will have straight smoke streams behind it.

You can use a hair dryer and ribbon instead of smoke to study how streamlined different shapes are.

Wind Tunnel

1 Make a backdrop for watching airstreams.

2 Cut slits in the side of a cereal box for the backdrop. Push two cardboard triangles through the slits.

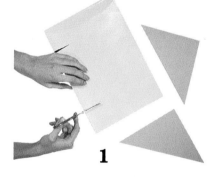

3 Carefully make holes through the center of the box and push two thin sticks through them. (These sticks will support shapes for testing, such as your airfoil and a ball.)

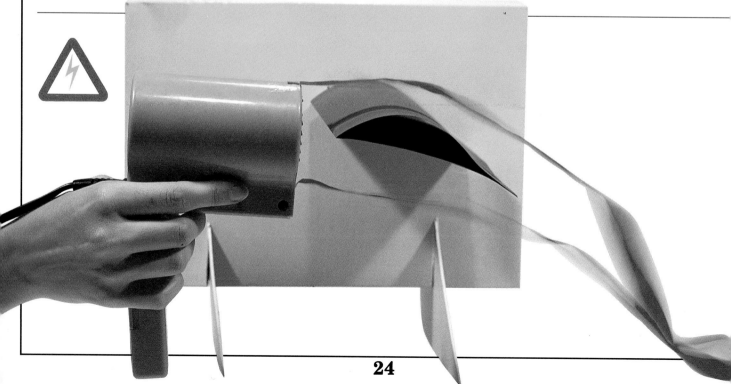

24

WHY IT WORKS

Your airfoil does not disrupt the lines of smoke – or the ribbons – as they pass over its surface. Instead, the smoke streams continue in almost the same lines as before they struck the wing. This means that the wing can move freely through the air. Air does not rub against it too much, slowing it down by air resistance. (Like water in a simming pool that seems to push us back if we walk through it, air resistance is a powerful force.)

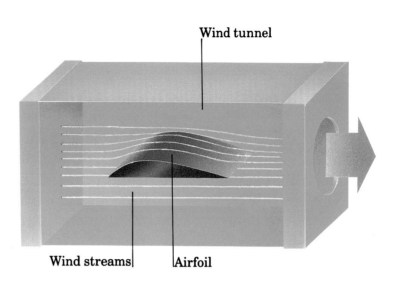

Wind tunnel

Wind streams   Airfoil

4 Tape two thin ribbons onto a hair dryer. With the dryer set on "cool," watch how the ribbons blow over your shapes to see the airstreams around them.

4

BRIGHT IDEAS

See how streams of air move around two different cars. Attach paper fronts to toy cars as shown below (see pages 20, 21). Stand each above a tabletop on a stick of modeling clay. Test each for streamlining.

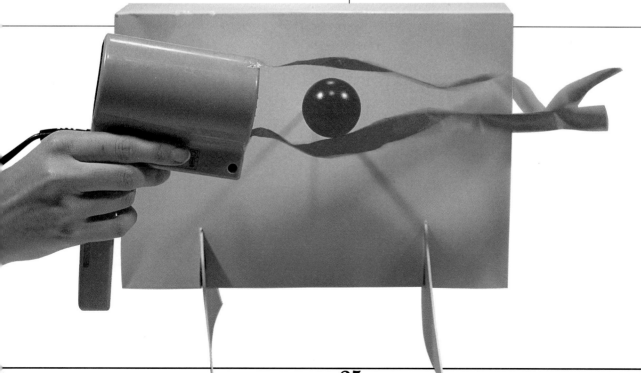

GLIDER FLIGHT

Have you seen a buzzard, a gull, or a kestrel in flight? At times some birds seem to hang in the air without having to flap their wings. Gliders copy these birds, floating on currents of rising air called thermals. Like kites, gliders fly without engine power. However, unlike hot-air balloons, gliders don't just follow the wind. A glider pilot can control the craft by using flaps on the tail and on the wings. The first glider to carry a person was built by an Englishman called Sir George Cayley, in 1853. A state-of-the-art glider, the Space Shuttle gets its lift from the airflow around it. You can make your own simple glider in the project below.

AIRCRAFT DESIGN

1 Study the photographs before you begin. The yellow strips show the flaps and the rudder. The white strips are for double-sided sticky tape.

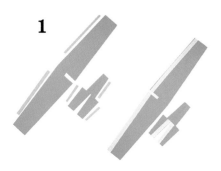

1

3 Tape on the yellow flaps. Feed a drinking straw through the wings to make an airfoil shape. Use a knitting needle for the body of the glider. Split a 2in piece of straw at one end, and tape it around the tail and onto the knitting needle.

2 Make the wings and tail from light, strong, thin oak tag. Cut out the two blue shapes and the five yellow flaps. Your glider can be whatever size you want.

2

3

BRIGHT IDEAS

Make your glider "roll." The wings give the glider stability – by moving the wing flaps you can shift its balance.

You can make your glider climb and dive by moving the flaps on the tail planes.

A pilot controls the "yaw" with the rudder on the tail. For a yaw to port (a turn to the left), set the rudder as in the picture below. Now try a yaw to starboard (a turn to the right) with your own rudder set as in the picture below.

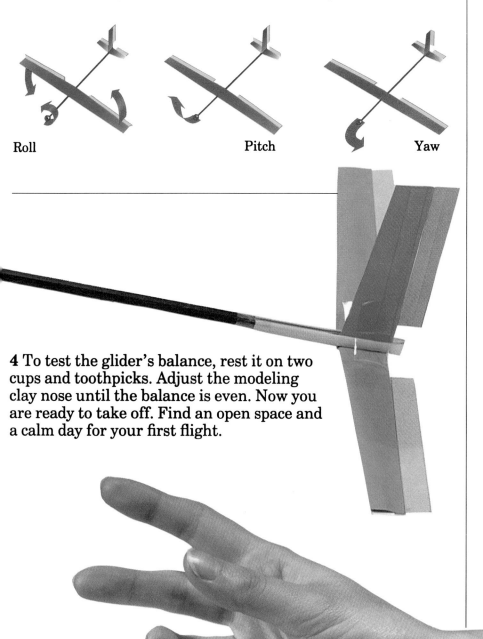

Roll

Pitch

Yaw

4 To test the glider's balance, rest it on two cups and toothpicks. Adjust the modeling clay nose until the balance is even. Now you are ready to take off. Find an open space and a calm day for your first flight.

WHY IT WORKS

Wings and tail flaps help to steer your aircraft. Depending on how these flaps are set (see Bright Ideas), your craft rolls, turns, climbs, or dives as pictured below. This is because the forward motion of the plane is redirected by the force of air hitting the tilted flaps.

Roll

Yaw

Pitch

PROPELLERS AND FANS

Have you ever heard a news report about a hurricane? The power of the wind can be very dangerous, destroying buildings and ripping up trees. If we catch the wind, it can be very helpful, too. Once, windmills used the wind's energy to drive grinding and threshing machinery. Today, smaller, modern windmills make electricity or pump water. The blades of a windmill use the same principle as airplanes, where the special shape of the wing makes them move smoothly in the air. Like sails on a boat, the blades can also turn to catch the wind from every direction.

WORKING WINDMILL

1 To put the power of the wind to work, begin by making holes in a juice carton as shown. Push two straws through the holes, with the bottom straw angling upward.

3

1

2 Make the blades for the propeller by following steps 1 to 3 of the whirligig project on page 30. You will need two pieces of 6in by 5in oak tag. Make the "tail" from the inside of a ballpoint pen.

2

3 Your windmill is going to turn a cam that will push a hammer up. The hammer will strike a table. Make these pieces from stiff cardboard as shown above.

5 To put your simple machine together push the propeller pen through the top straw. The cam wire feeds into this straw from the back.

5

4 Tape the L-shaped wire to the yellow cam. Pierce a small hole in the center of the hammer, push the other wire through, and tape it down. Now fold up the "head" of the hammer.

4

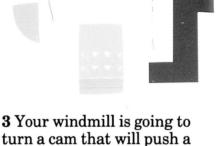

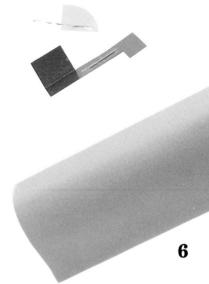

6

6 The hammer wire feeds into the high end of the bottom straw. Press some modeling clay onto the head. Tape on the table. Now blow on the blades and start your windmill spinning.

28

BRIGHT IDEAS

☀ Blow on your windmill at different angles as shown here. See which direction makes the blades turn the most quickly and smoothly.

☀ To make a simple paper windmill, you need a square piece of oak tag. Decorate both sides. Cut diagonally from each corner, stopping one-third of the way from the center. Fold down every other point and secure them in the center with a pin. Push the pin through a bead before attaching it to a stick.

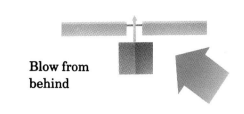

Blow from behind

Blow on side

Blow from front

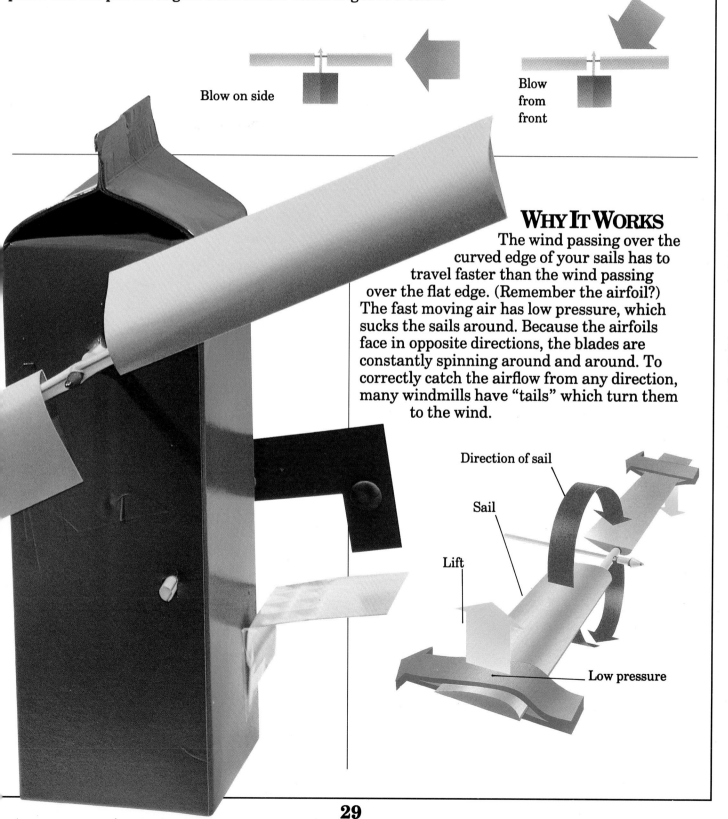

WHY IT WORKS

The wind passing over the curved edge of your sails has to travel faster than the wind passing over the flat edge. (Remember the airfoil?) The fast moving air has low pressure, which sucks the sails around. Because the airfoils face in opposite directions, the blades are constantly spinning around and around. To correctly catch the airflow from any direction, many windmills have "tails" which turn them to the wind.

Direction of sail

Sail

Lift

Low pressure

HELICOPTER ACTION

As any object falls through the air, the air pushes against it. Many trees have winged seeds that use this push to make them spin. The wings are shaped like airfoils, so as they spin they stir up low pressure above them. Higher pressure from the blanket of air below slows their fall as they drift away from the "parent tree." Helicopters also get lift from twirling airfoils. Their rotor blades spin so hard that the low pressure creates enough lift to carry them into the air.

WHIRLIGIG

1 Make two small airfoils from two pieces of oak tag, 4in by 3in. Fold each piece with an overlap.

1

2 Push the overlapping edges together and tape them together. One side will curve up like a wing.

2

3

3 Spread a little glue onto each end of a stiff straw or thin stick. With the curved side of the wings pointing up, glue them onto the straw so that they face in different directions.

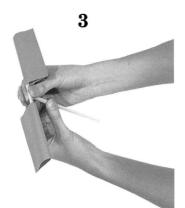

4

4 Tape another straw to the one holding the wings. Use a piece of modeling clay to weigh down the end. This keeps the whirligig level.

5 To send the whirligig spinning, hold it between the palms of your hands. Brush your hands together, pulling one toward you and pushing the other away. As your hands come apart, the whirligig is released, twirling as it flies.

5

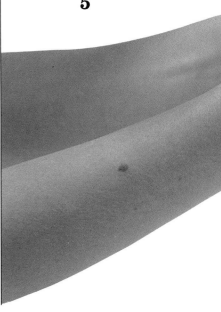

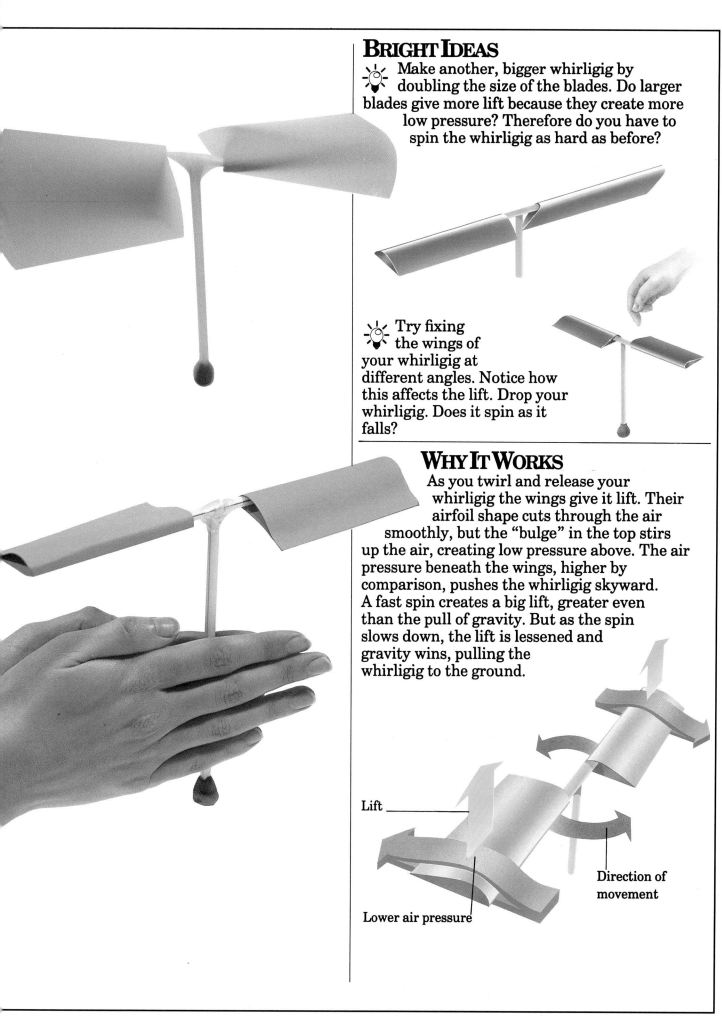

BRIGHT IDEAS

Make another, bigger whirligig by doubling the size of the blades. Do larger blades give more lift because they create more low pressure? Therefore do you have to spin the whirligig as hard as before?

Try fixing the wings of your whirligig at different angles. Notice how this affects the lift. Drop your whirligig. Does it spin as it falls?

WHY IT WORKS

As you twirl and release your whirligig the wings give it lift. Their airfoil shape cuts through the air smoothly, but the "bulge" in the top stirs up the air, creating low pressure above. The air pressure beneath the wings, higher by comparison, pushes the whirligig skyward. A fast spin creates a big lift, greater even than the pull of gravity. But as the spin slows down, the lift is lessened and gravity wins, pulling the whirligig to the ground.

Lift

Direction of movement

Lower air pressure

SCIENTIFIC TERMS

AIRFOIL A surface, like an aircraft wing, which is shaped to produce lift when air flows over and under it

ATMOSPHERE The layer of air that surrounds the earth

BAROMETER An instrument that measures changes in air pressure used to predict the weather

CONVECTION CURRENTS Movements of hot and cold air

DRAG Air resistance, a force that holds back moving objects

EDDIES Moving ripples of air

FRICTION A force between two objects that rub together, which slows things down

GRAVITY The pull of the earth that gives things weight

LATEEN A triangular sail that allows a boat to sail against the wind

LIFT An upward force created by low pressure above

OXYGEN A gas that makes up one-fifth of the air and is essential to life

PITCH A turn upward or downward of the nose of an aircraft

PRESSURE The force exerted on the surface of the earth by the atmosphere due to the gravitational pull of the earth

ROLL A tipping of the wings of an aircraft in which one tips upward and the other tips downward

STREAMLINING Making an object smooth and rounded so that air flows easily over its surface

THERMALS Currents of rising air

YAW A turn from an aircraft's straight course

INDEX

PRINTED IN BELGIUM BY
proost
INTERNATIONAL BOOK PRODUCTION